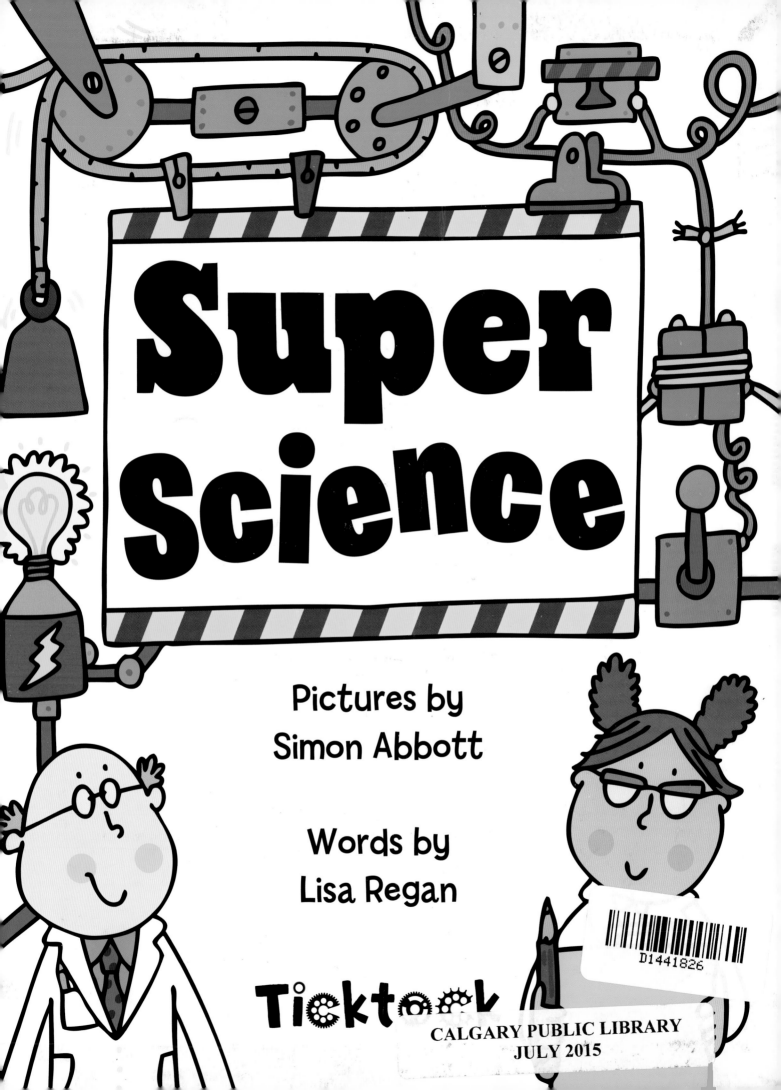

Super Science

Pictures by
Simon Abbott

Words by
Lisa Regan

Ticktock

Tiny Stuff

The world of science is all around us. It affects big things, like inventions and exploring space. But it starts with very, very tiny things – much too small to see.

Everything is made of tiny things called **atoms**. The human eye can only see things the size of a pinpoint. To study atoms and other supersmall objects, scientists use microscopes, which can make things appear **2,000** times bigger.

I spy, with my little eye...

7,000,000,000,000,00

Write down a 7 with **27 zeros** and that's how many of these teeny tiny atoms make up your **body**!

If you look at **snow crystals** using a microscope, you can see that each one has six main arms. No two crystals are ever the same!

,000,000,000,000

Brrrrrrr!

Did You Know?
Bacteria are tiny living things – millions of them would fit on the head of a pin.

It's a tight squeeze!

Yogurt is made by adding bacteria to milk. Yum!

WOW!

The atoms in your body were formed at the start of the universe, so really you're **billions** of years old!

What's the Matter?

Atoms all join together to make stuff. Scientists call this stuff "matter." They usually describe matter as solid, liquid, or gas.

Liquid matter pours and spills, and will flow away unless it is kept in a container.

Ooooops!

Oh, nuts!

Solid matter has its own shape, like a bike or a cake.

FUN FACTS

Bread rises because bubbles of **carbon dioxide** form as it bakes.

Make the most of your party balloons – **helium gas**, used to make balloons float, is running out!

Gas spreads out in the air around us. It is usually invisible but often has a smell.

Carbon dioxide is a very important **gas**. We breathe it out, and trees and plants breathe it in. It is also what makes a fizzy drink fizzy!

Water can be all three types of matter. It is **liquid** when you drink it, **solid** when it freezes into ice, and **gas** when it boils and becomes steam.

Let's break the ice!

The atoms released by **flowers** and **fruits** float into your nose, giving them their different smells!

WOW!

Boom!

Reactions are important in science. They happen when something changes, like wood being burned by a flame. Imagine being a caveman and discovering fire!

Some reactions give off energy – **light**, **sound**, or **heat**. When a firework goes off, it makes all three!

I think they're done!

MARSHMALLOWS

Reactions can be **slow**. If you were to leave your bike outside for a long time, it would get **rusty**. But they can be fast, too, like the inside of an apple turning brown once you've bitten into it.

A **rocket** needs a reaction to fly –
mixing **liquid hydrogen** (say hyde-roh-jen) and
liquid oxygen (say ox-ee-jen) makes it blast into the air!

...and just shake...

HYDROGEN

OXYGEN

Feel the Force

Forces are things that move or change objects, such as pushing, pulling, and squashing. Forces can make things speed up or slow down.

Forces happen in different directions. If forces are the same size but in opposite directions, they balance each other out.

Watch out!

If two people push a skateboard from opposite ends with **equal force**, the skateboard will stay still. If one person uses more force, the skateboard will move.

Strike!

A **bowling ball** rolls along until it **hits** the pins. The force knocks them over.

Magnets have an invisible force around them called **magnetism**, which **pulls** metal towards them. That's why a paper clip seems to "stick" to a magnet.

I'm irresistible!

The air around us produces a force called **air resistance**. It slows things down as they move. Racing cars and airplanes are designed to have less air resistance and can move faster.

Out of this world!

On Earth, a force called **gravity** pulls everything downwards and stops us floating away. Gravity exists on the moon, but it's not as strong. That's why astronauts seem to bounce on the moon's surface.

Bright Sparks!

Electricity is a very important kind of energy. It is invisible, but we can see the things it does, such as making televisions, computers, and lights work!

Electricity flows along wires into your home. When you plug things in, you supply electricity to them. The electricity can then be turned into other kinds of energy, like **heat** from a hair dryer and **sound** from a radio.

Scientists have known about electricity for hundreds of years, but they only found ways of using it beginning in the 1800s. Before then, **candles** were used for light, **wood** was burned for heat, and ice kept things cool.

One **lightbulb** gives off the same light as around **25,000 fireflies!**

Some **eels** can make their own electricity to give a shock to their enemies.

Electricity can be made by burning fuel, like **gas** and **oil**.

These fuels are running out, so it's important to make electricity in other ways, such as with **wind turbines** and **solar panels**.

Batteries, such as those in cell phones and toys, store electricity so it can be carried where it is needed.

The **International Space Station** uses lots of solar panels to make its own electricity in space.

WOW!

Living Things

Scientists called biologists (say bye-ol-o-gists) study how living things work. They look at plants and animals to find out more about how they eat, move, and grow.

I'm feeling a little hungry.

Animals need fuel to survive. Food is their **fuel**, and an animal's body turns it into **energy** so it can breathe, find more food, and have babies.

Yum!

Humans are animals, too. We get our food from **plants** and other **animals** (which give us meat, milk, and eggs).

I'll have a steak sandwich... and make it snappy!

Plants make their own food using **sunlight**. That's why plants don't need to walk around to find things to eat!

Breathe in... and breathe out!

Many living creatures need **air** to breathe. The air contains **oxygen**, and the oxygen is used to change the food we eat into energy – so that we can move and do things.

Fish and other underwater creatures get their oxygen from the water. They have **gills** on their sides, which take in the oxygen.

Did You Know?
The world's **biggest creature**, the blue whale, eats one of the **smallest**: krill.

Dolphins don't drink water. They get all the water they need from their food.

WOW!

About **one quarter** of all living creatures on Earth are **beetles**.

BEETLE POWER!

That's Better!

If you're sick, medicine can often help you get well again. Medicines can be used to cure diseases or to help your body work better.

We're sometimes given **immunizations** (say im-you-nize-zay-shuns) to stop us getting sick. They put a teeny bit of a **disease** into your body, which helps fight off the actual disease.

Your body is home to millions of **bacteria**. Some bacteria can make you sick but most are harmless and some even help your body to work.

Ready for my shot, doc!

FUN FACTS

Hundreds of years ago, surgery was often done by the local **barber**!

How much do you want off?

Your nose produces new **mucus** (snot!) every 20 minutes.

Penicillin (say pen-i-sil-in) is a medicine used to kill unwanted bacteria. It comes from a type of mold, which **Alexander Fleming** discovered by accident when he left out dirty lab equipment - which turned moldy!

Doctors can send samples of your blood, pee, or poop to a **laboratory**. Scientists look at them under a **microscope** to find out what's making you sick.

This has me in stitches!

Finding a new **medicine** and making sure it is safe to use takes at least 10 years.

Add a little bit of that...

WOW!

Around Planet Earth

From Earth we can look up and see many amazing things around us: clouds, the sun, the moon, stars, and other planets.

The Earth is round, which means you can see **different stars** depending on where you are. A person in Australia can't see the stars that someone in America can.

The Earth is surrounded by a thin layer of gases called the **atmosphere**. This **protects** the Earth from the sun's rays and keeps our planet at the right **temperature** for things to live.

I feel dizzy!

We can't feel it, but the Earth is always **spinning**. In the 1500s, a scientist called **Copernicus** (say koh-pur-ni-kus) told people that our planet was traveling **around the sun**.

Not many people believed him at first, but it's **true**!

What a view!

The **clouds** that make our weather are in the bottom layer of the atmosphere. A cloud is made of billions of tiny drops of **water** and **ice**.

Inventions Everywhere

Science lies behind all of the clever things we use every day, from a pair of scissors to a telephone.

The Egyptians used simple machines like **levers** and **ramps** to help them build the pyramids. The wheel hadn't been invented yet, so they couldn't use carts.

Hair today... gone tomorrow!

A simple pair of **scissors** has different parts: the blades for cutting and a pair of **levers** to increase the force from the blades.

FUN FACTS

A type of superfast train, called a **maglev**, has no wheels but floats above the tracks using magnets.

A **telephone** changes the sound of your voice into **electrical signals** that can travel along a wire. The wires even run under the sea so you can phone people in other countries!

Cell phones work in a similar way, but the electrical signals are sent through the air. Tall poles (called cell towers) work like antennae to collect the signals and send them to the person you are talking to!

An American called **Thomas Edison** invented over 1,000 things, including the **electric lightbulb**, which works when electricity flows through a thin wire in the bulb. This wire gets so hot that it glows and gives off light.

Some parts of the rockets that first took people to the **moon** are still floating in space.

Scientists have invented a car that is powered by gas from **human poop!**

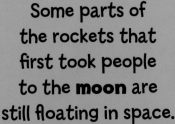

Pee-ew!

WOW!

Super Science Facts

Most liquids shrink
when they freeze, but water
gets **bigger** when it turns to ice.

Thunderclouds store **electrical energy**
and release it as flashes of lightning.

It can take an **hour** for
a snowflake to reach
the ground from
a cloud!

X-rays (waves of a kind of light)
pass right through skin and muscle,
but not through solid bone. That's
how a doctor can "see" inside your
body to check your bones.

Karl Benz invented one of the first cars,
in 1886. It used gas as a fuel to make
energy to drive the engine. During test
drives, he was told off for scaring
children with the loud noise!